Maps AND Mapping

MAPPING
THE WEATHER

BY
JOHN WOOD

KidHaven
PUBLISHING

Published in 2020 by KidHaven Publishing, an Imprint of Greenhaven Publishing, LLC
353 3rd Avenue, Suite 255, New York, NY 10010

Written by: John Wood
Edited by: Kirsty Holmes
Designed by: Gareth Liddington

Cataloging-in-Publication Data

Names: Wood, John.
Title: Mapping weather / John Wood.
Description: New York : KidHaven Publishing, 2020. | Series: Maps and mapping | Includes glossary and index.
Identifiers: ISBN 9781534531130 (pbk.) | ISBN 9781534530249 (library bound) | ISBN 9781534531543 (6 pack) | ISBN 9781534531079 (ebook)
Subjects: LCSH: Weather--Maps--Juvenile literature. | Weather--Juvenile literature. | Map reading--Juvenile literature.
Classification: LCC QC981.3 W66 2020 | DDC 551.5--dc23

Image Credits
All images are courtesy of Shutterstock.com, unless otherwise specified. With thanks to Getty Images, Thinkstock Photo and iStockphoto.
Front Cover – Iafoto, Vasin Lee. 4&5 – Rawpixel.com, Rainer Lesniewski, D1min, Andrey_Popov, Sentavio. 6&7 – solarseven, Hannes Grobe, Famartin, Ekaphon maneechot, Designua, 8&9 – Andrey Bermakin, Aleksei Sharazev, susumis, Michal Belka, iceink, 10&11 – Rainer Lesniewski, Lavinia Bordea, ZoranOrcik, Pilvitus, Morphart Creation, 12&13 – Bardocz Tamas, NOAA, igorstevanovic, Martyman, KVDP. 14&15 – Rainer Lesniewski, Liudacorolewa, TonyCohen, Ori~. 16&17 – APHITHANA, Galyna Andrushko, Designua. 18&19 – Trong Nguyen, NASA images, Miami2you, Jacqueline F Cooper, FEMA personnel. 20&21 – Yaska, Jeff Gammons Storm Visuals, NOAA. 22&23 – Lars Christensen, wikimedia, cpaulfell, Bjarki Sigursveinsson, hektoR. 24&25 – Zacarias Pereira da Mata, Emoscopes, pfly, John D Sirlin. 26&27 – Kolonko, Arto Hakola, Derek Ramsey, Gertjan Hooijer, Dr Ajay Kumar Singh. 28&29 – NASA, Victor Maschek, Zul Kefli, FotograFFF, Vadim Sadovski. 30 – National Weather Service, Vangert, Anna Utkina, Eric Isselee.

Printed in the United States of America

CPSIA compliance information: Batch #BS19KL: For further information contact Greenhaven Publishing LLC, New York, New York at 1-844-317-7404.

CONTENTS

Words that look like **this** are explained in the glossary on page 31.

WHAT ARE MAPS FOR?

What Is a Map?

Maps are diagrams that show parts of the world and how they are connected. Maps can show a big area, like the entire world, or a small area, like a town or village. Some maps only show natural **features** of the landscape, like mountains and rivers. Other maps show where buildings and roads are. Some maps only show specific things, like amusement park maps, which are for visitors to find their way around a park and plan their day.

With this map, a visitor can see where all the rides and roller coasters are and how to get to each one.

BY NOT INCLUDING OTHER INFORMATION, THE MAP OF AFRICA IS EASIER TO READ.

CHOOSING WHAT TO MAP

A mapmaker, called a cartographer, often can't put all parts of an area on a map. Because some things are left out, or simplified, a map doesn't always look exactly like a place. It is a drawing instead of a photo. Maps are useful to see certain features, **landmarks**, people, vegetation, or animals. The finished map can show some of these things clearly, but can't show everything, so they have to choose what is important.

This map of Africa only shows some natural features, like vegetation, and not towns or cities.

GEOGRAPHIC MAPS

Different maps are used for different reasons. Maps of the climate show what kind of weather is expected for a certain time of year, whereas weather maps predict the weather today or tomorrow. Road maps show drivers where to go, while a terrain map traces the rises and falls of the land. A political map shows the size of different countries and where the borders between them are. These types of maps are all geographic, which means they map the Earth and its features.

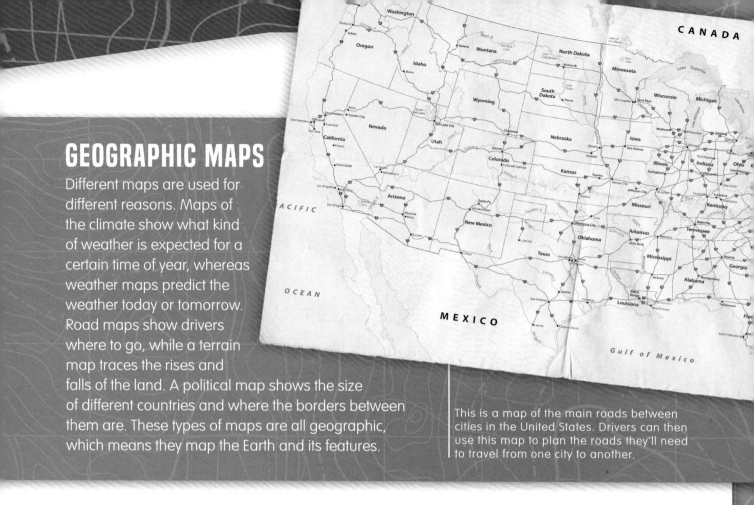

This is a map of the main roads between cities in the United States. Drivers can then use this map to plan the roads they'll need to travel from one city to another.

Non-Geographic Maps

There are even maps of objects and things that aren't part of the landscape. There are tree maps that show the order of events and how they are related. For example, a family tree shows how people are related to each other. Mind maps are ways to come up with ideas that are linked to one main topic. The police use maps that link different pieces of **evidence** together to work out how a crime was committed.

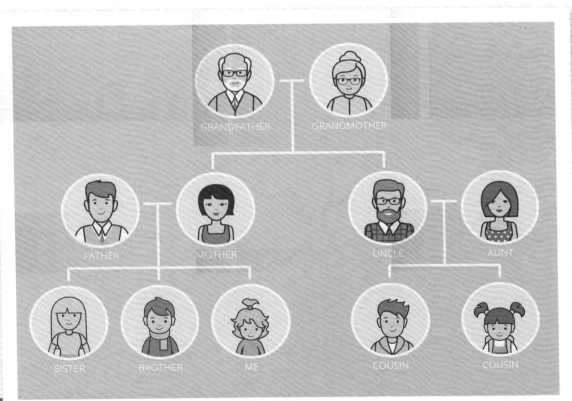

Putting related topics or items together in one place can help us to understand how they are linked and to make new connections.

CLIMATE AND WEATHER

The weather outside might be warm and sunny, or cold and rainy. It usually depends on the country and what time of year it is. Weather can change at any moment. Climate is the word we use to describe the **average** weather in a place over a period of time.

Some air is heated as it goes over cities or warm parts of the ocean.

What Causes Weather?

The air on Earth is also called the atmosphere. The atmosphere is everywhere, from the ground to the sky. However, the air isn't the same everywhere. In some areas, the air might be warm, and in others it might be cold. When warm and cold air **interact** with each other, it causes all the things we call weather, such as rain, snow, wind, and clouds.

Because the Earth is round and **tilted**, it is not heated evenly by the sun. This means some parts of the atmosphere are warmer than others.

Equator

Sun

WHAT GOES UP...

Warm air becomes lighter and rises. Cooler air from all around rushes in to replace the warm air that has floated upward. If the rising air becomes colder, it will become heavier, and sink back down to the surface of the Earth. The rising and falling creates a movement of air around the world, which causes wind and weather.

AS THE AIR RISES AND FALLS, THE WATER IN THE AIR HEATS AND COOLS. THIS CAN CAUSE IT TO TURN FROM WATER VAPOR INTO LIQUID WATER. THE LIQUID WATER FALLS FROM THE SKY AS RAIN.

HOW DO WE MEASURE WEATHER?

To put weather on a map, scientists must first measure the movements of air and changes in temperature. **Satellites** can be used to track this information from space. The satellites use instruments, such as **radiometers**, to collect information about the clouds, atmosphere, and temperature of the air.

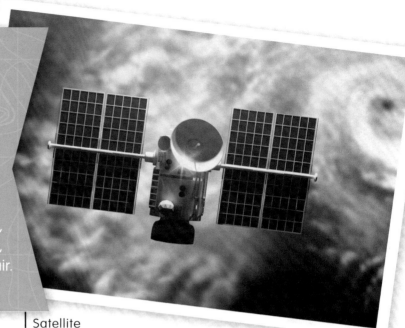

Satellite

Places that detect changes in the weather are often called weather stations. Many weather stations gather information using something called a radiosonde. A radiosonde is a device that measures information about temperature, air movement, and the amount of water in the air. Radiosondes are tied to large balloons, which float high into the atmosphere. Some weather stations launch two of these every day!

A Radiosonde Attached to a Weather Balloon

An ASOS in Nevada

Automated Surface Observing Systems (ASOS) are stations on the ground full of machines that work automatically, without anyone looking after them. ASOS looks into the sky and takes measurements about the clouds, rain, temperature, and wind. Information gathered about weather is sent to be studied by scientists and supercomputers.

THE WEATHER FORECAST

Umbrellas or Sunscreen?

Unlike other maps, most weather maps do not show us what has already been found. Weather maps are all about what we are going to find in the future. A prediction of what the weather is going to be like is called a weather forecast. Weather forecasts are easily found on the Internet and they are often shown on television. Usually a weather presenter will stand in front of a map of a country with special symbols and information about tomorrow's weather.

TYPICALLY, 5-DAY WEATHER FORECASTS ACCURATELY PREDICT THE WEATHER ABOUT 90% OF THE TIME.

Different countries will use different weather stations for the forecast. Because each station has collected its own data, the forecast may be slightly different between countries. Forecasts might also change because scientists get new information about the atmosphere, which can change their weather prediction. Although the weather forecast might not always come true, most predictions are very accurate due to the complicated scientific instruments and supercomputers that collect and study the information.

Sunny

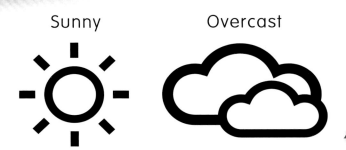

Overcast

SYMBOLS

A weather forecast map will have symbols that show different types of weather. Here are a few weather symbols you might see:

Thunderstorm   Clear Night   Cloudy with Sun   Snow

Symbols with Exciting Numbers

The weather map may also show the wind speed and direction. These symbols will look like numbers in a circle with an arrow. The arrow shows the direction and the number shows how many miles (or kilometers) the wind is traveling per hour.

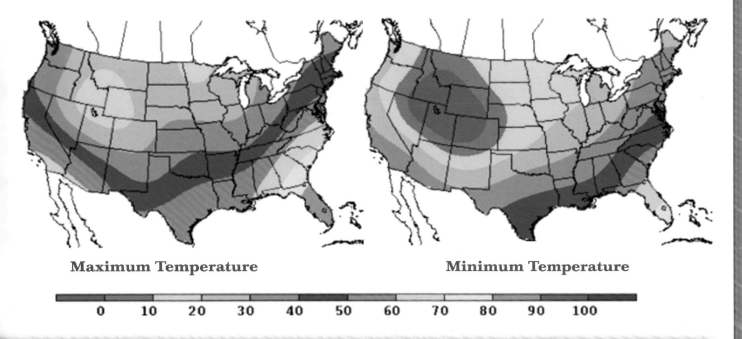

Maximum Temperature   **Minimum Temperature**

0   10   20   30   40   50   60   70   80   90   100

The weather presenter may also show the temperature. The map might be full of circles with numbers in them. The numbers will show how many degrees **Fahrenheit** or **Celsius** the temperature will be. There may also be colors to show how hot it is. Orange and red usually means it is very hot, while yellow usually means it is warm. Blue usually means it is freezing cold.

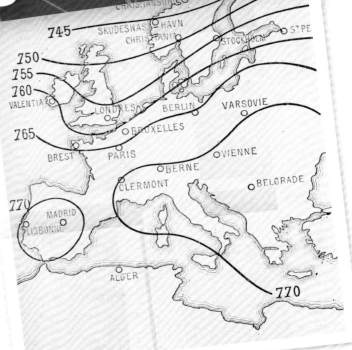

Isolines and Isobars

Some maps group areas together with lines called isolines. Isolines can clearly show areas that are similar to each other in some way. Weather maps often use a type of isoline called an isobar. Isobars show areas where the air has a certain temperature and pressure. Warm, light air creates low pressure on the ground, whereas cold, heavy air creates high pressure. The more isobars there are in one place, the bigger the difference in pressure. A bigger difference will probably cause more wind and bad weather.

Isobars might have a number showing the amount of pressure in an area. Instead of a number, these areas may instead have an H (high pressure) or an L (low pressure).

COLD FRONTS AND WARM FRONTS

The boundary between warm air and cold air is called a front. There are many types of fronts, and each has a different symbol on a weather map. Cold fronts and warm fronts are the most common.

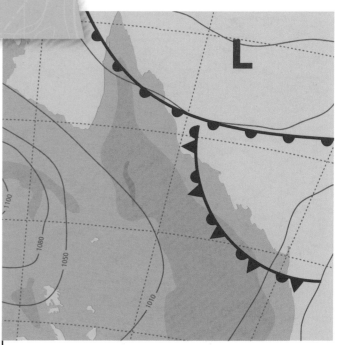

Cold fronts are lines with blue spikes. This means an area of cold, heavy air is coming in and scooping the warm air upward.

Warm fronts are lines with red semicircles. This means an area of warm, light air is rising up over the edge of colder air.

RAIN OR SHINE

Tracking these fronts and putting them on a weather map can show what kind of weather is going to happen. A cold front often brings gusty winds, heavy rain, and **storms**. A warm front will probably bring high, thin clouds first, and perhaps light rain later. Depending on the temperature difference, the weather may be more or less severe. For example, if the warm air is very hot and the cold air is very cold, there will be a much bigger difference in temperature. This difference will cause heavier rain or bigger storms.

A map with isobars, hot fronts, and cold fronts

Back to the Drawing Board

It is impossible to know what kind of a front will form until warm air and cold air meet. Once the fronts form, they can be put on a map. Weather stations need to regularly track the weather and update their forecasts because fronts can change at any time. Weather maps are **temporary** and often change, just like the weather.

Weather Station

CHOROPLETH
MAPS

Coloring in with Cartographers

A choropleth map is not used to find your way around. Instead of showing roads, rivers, towns, or cities, a choropleth map uses colors to show one type of information about a place. For example, choropleth maps might be used to show the climate. These kinds of maps will have a **key** to show what each color means. On a climate map, blue might mean a cold, snowy climate. All the places in the world that have that kind of climate would be colored in blue.

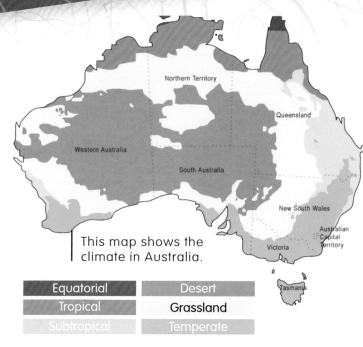

This map shows the climate in Australia.

Equatorial	Desert
Tropical	Grassland
Subtropical	Temperate

Choropleth maps are often used to show temperature. The key will usually use colors like red and yellow for hot temperatures, and blue and white for cold temperatures. Temperature maps of the world are useful for seeing how temperature is unevenly spread out across the globe. The middle of the world, around the **equator**, is much hotter. This area is called the tropics. The top and bottom of the world are called poles, and they are much colder.

THE HEAT OF THE TROPICS IS MOVED AROUND THE WORLD BY OCEANS AND THE MOVEMENT OF AIR.

Tropic of Cancer | Tropic of Capricorn | The area between the two tropical lines is called the tropics. All countries in this area will have hot, tropical climates.

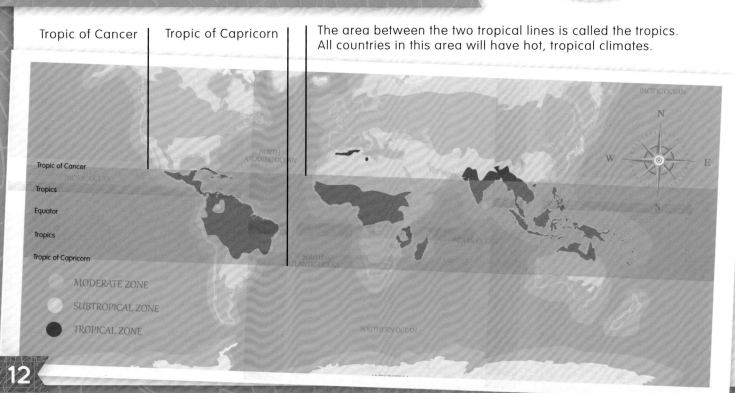

Unlike a weather map, choropleth maps can show weather that has happened in the past. It is possible to collect lots of these maps together and see how they change over time. For example, maps that show rainfall in a certain place can be compared over time to see if the amount changes. When people want to show the effects of climate change, they often use maps from different times to show the rises in temperature or the melting of sea ice.

This map uses color to show the amount of rainfall.

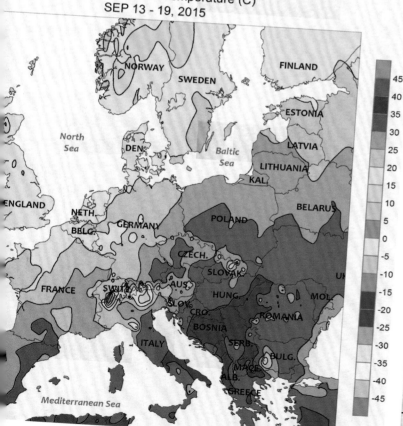

Off the Chart

In 2013, Australia's Bureau of Meteorology had to add a new color to its temperature maps. A temperature of over 125.6°F (52°C) was recorded, which was higher than ever before. There was no color for that on their key, so a purple color was added to show this new temperature. Because of climate change, there will be many new records set in the future for all sorts of things, such as the amount of storms, rainfall, and increase in sea level.

Temperature Map

THE GREAT OCEAN CONVEYOR BELT

Maps for Movement

Some maps need to track the flow of something. These types of maps might use flow lines or arrows to show the direction of flow and movement. The size of the arrow can show the strength of the flow.

This map shows the movement of trade to and from the United States of America.

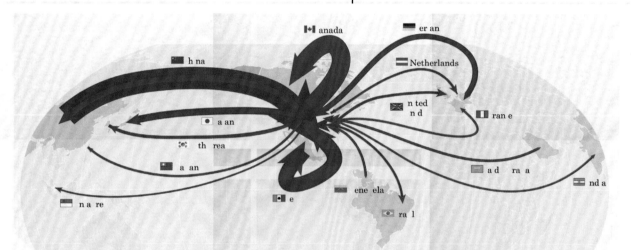

Canada
China
Japan
South Korea
Japan
Singapore
Germany
Netherlands
United Kingdom
France
Australia
India
Mexico
Venezuela
Brazil

THE GREAT OCEAN CONVEYOR BELT

A very important part of the weather cycle is the Great Ocean Conveyor Belt. These are the large ocean **currents** that move heat around the world. The Great Ocean Conveyor Belt can be mapped using flow lines and arrows. This flow of water is caused by cold water sinking to the bottom of the ocean at the poles of the Earth. The water around fills the sinking water, and this is what starts this worldwide flow of water. The cold water, which has sunk to the bottom, travels to the equator and rises to complete the cycle.

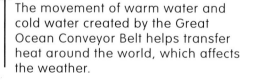

The movement of warm water and cold water created by the Great Ocean Conveyor Belt helps transfer heat around the world, which affects the weather.

THE GREAT OCEAN CONVEYOR BELT MOVES A LOT OF WATER VERY SLOWLY. WATER THAT MOVES IN THIS CIRCUIT MOVES ABOUT 0.4 INCH (1 CM) PER SECOND.

As the world gets warmer and the ice caps melt, the melted ice water might stop the cold water from sinking and being replaced by warm, tropical water. This will affect the weather and temperatures in other parts of the world, especially north-western Europe.

THE GULF STREAM

The Gulf Stream is part of the Great Ocean Conveyor Belt. It is one of the strongest currents in any of the oceans. The Gulf Stream starts in the Gulf of Mexico and flows through the Atlantic Ocean, passing the eastern coastline of North America. Maps of the Gulf Stream usually have arrows to show the direction of the current. Arrows may also be different colors to show different temperatures of the water. Red often means warm water and blue often means cold water.

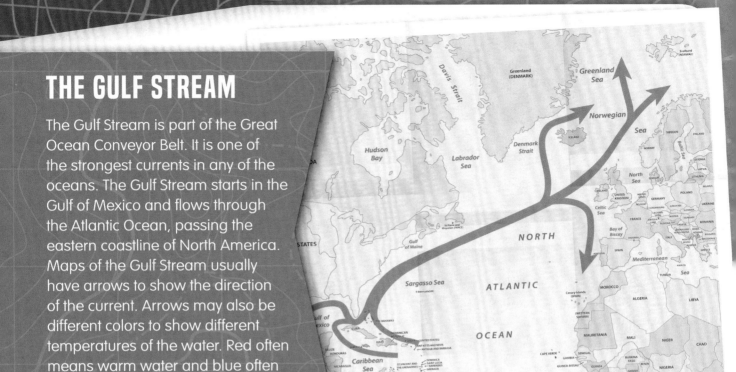

A Map of the Gulf Stream

Franklin Gets His Maps Out

Benjamin Franklin wondered why some ships could travel to America so much faster than others. After talking to other sailors and whalers, Franklin found out about a "warm, strong current" that the ships rode along. He **charted** the route of this current, and became the first person to map the route of the Gulf Stream.

Benjamin Franklin

THE GULF STREAM MOVES A LOT OF HEAT FROM THE TROPICS TO THE TOP OF THE ATLANTIC AND EUROPE. THIS GIVES NORTH-WESTERN EUROPE A MUCH WARMER CLIMATE THAN IT WOULD USUALLY HAVE.

EL NIÑO AND LA NIÑA

El Niño

El Niño (say: El Neen-yo) is the name for a rise in water temperature in the Pacific Ocean that affects weather patterns all over the world. El Niño is Spanish for "little boy," which is a reference to the birth of Jesus Christ. It is called this because the weather changes caused by El Niño usually happen around Christmastime.

Usually, in winter, the warmest water is found near South America and is pushed westward toward Indonesia by strong winds. However, during El Niño, winds are weaker and the warm water stays nearer South America. This warm water **evaporates** and forms storm clouds that cause dramatic weather, such as hurricanes and flooding. El Niño only happens every few years and it tends to bring heavy rainfall to countries in South America such as Ecuador and Peru. El Niño has been known to cause monsoons in Southeast Asia, flooding in Mexico, and droughts in Australia.

NORMAL YEAR

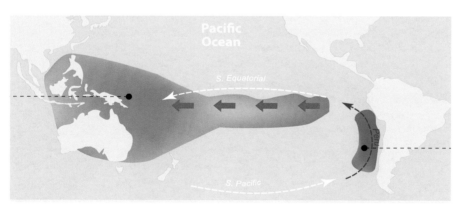

Equatorial winds gather. Warm water pools towards the west.

Cold water along South American coast

EL NIÑO YEAR

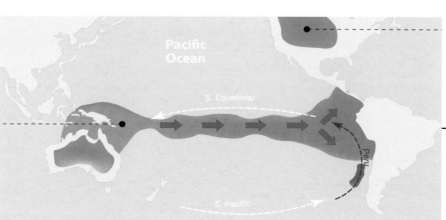

Easterly winds weaken. Warm water moves eastward.

Warmer winter

A map showing the direction that warm water travels during a normal year and an El Niño year.

LA NIÑA

The opposite of El Niño is when the water in the Pacific Ocean gets colder than usual. Because it is the opposite of El Niño, it gets called La Niña (say: La Neen-ya), which is Spanish for "little girl." La Niña causes fewer rain clouds to form so weather is usually drier in southern parts of the U.S. such as Texas, Arizona, and New Mexico. However, La Niña can cause more hurricanes to form in the Atlantic Ocean on the east coast of the U.S.

Thermal maps can show us the difference between ocean temperatures during an El Niño and a La Niña. The blue and green colors show cold temperatures while the reds and oranges show warm temperatures. Can you tell which one of these maps shows El Niño and which shows La Niña?

 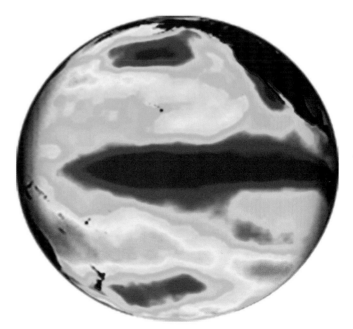

SEA SURFACE TEMPERATURE ANOMALY (⁰C) THERMAL MAP

-4   -2   0   2   4

TROPICAL CYCLONES

Extreme Weather

A tropical cyclone is a huge, dangerous storm. These storms have different names depending on where in the world they are created. In the Atlantic and northeast Pacific, these storms are called hurricanes. In the Northwest Pacific they are called typhoons, and in the southern Pacific and Indian Oceans they are called cyclones.

THE WIND SPEEDS INSIDE A TROPICAL CYCLONE USUALLY REACH SPEEDS OF AROUND 74.5 MILES (120 KM) AN HOUR.

This is a tropical cyclone seen from above.

THERE'S A STORM BREWING...

Tropical cyclones are formed in the same way as other storms. Warm, wet air rises, and air from all around rushes in to fill the space. The air that rushes in then rises, and the cycle repeats, again and again. However, tropical cyclones are much more powerful and deadly than other storms, and they only form in the tropics. This is because the high temperature in the tropics creates more rising, warm air. The ocean surface needs to be at least 80.6°F (27°C) to form a tropical storm. Because the Earth spins, the rising air also moves around in a spiral. This creates a storm of swirling, dangerous wind and rain, which can travel long distances around the world.

The center of a tropical cyclone is called the eye. Unlike the rest of the storm, the eye is quiet and calm. It is formed by cold air sinking in the middle of the storm.

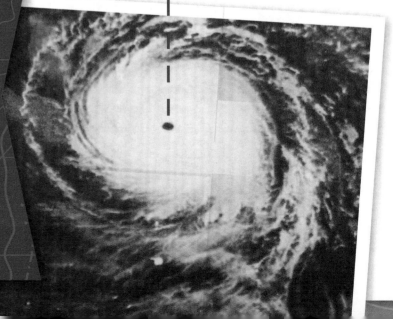

Plotting the Path

When a tropical cyclone forms, weather stations might give the storm a name to make it clearer and easier to talk about. The storm is then tracked by satellites, **radar**, and special aircraft. Scientists feed the information they gathered about the storm into a computer, which can make predictions about where the storm will go next. The storm's route is **plotted** on a map, and may be shown on weather reports and forecasts. These maps are important because they allow people to get out of the way of the storm if it is heading for their homes.

Hurricane Irma in Florida

This is a picture of the damage caused by Hurricane Harvey in Texas.

THE LARGEST TROPICAL CYCLONE EVER RECORDED WAS TYPHOON TIP, IN 1979. TYPHOON TIP HAD WIND SPEEDS OF 190 MILES (306 KM) PER HOUR, AND WAS 1,380 MILES (2,220 KM) WIDE.

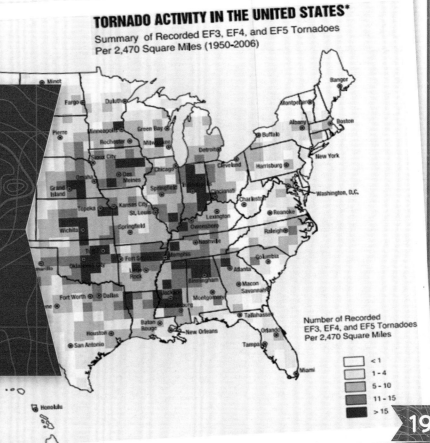

TORNADO ALLEY

Tornado Alley is an area that stretches from South Dakota to Texas in the United States. Tornadoes are common in this area because of the warm air from the Gulf of Mexico mixing with cold air from the Rocky Mountain Range. Over 1,000 tornadoes happen every year. Although the area can be shown on a map, the exact position of the tornadoes is hard to predict.

TORNADO ACTIVITY IN THE UNITED STATES*
Summary of Recorded EF3, EF4, and EF5 Tornadoes Per 2,470 Square Miles (1950-2006)

Number of Recorded EF3, EF4, and EF5 Tornadoes Per 2,470 Square Miles

< 1
1 - 4
5 - 10
11 - 15
> 15

A Map of Tornado Alley

STORM CHASERS

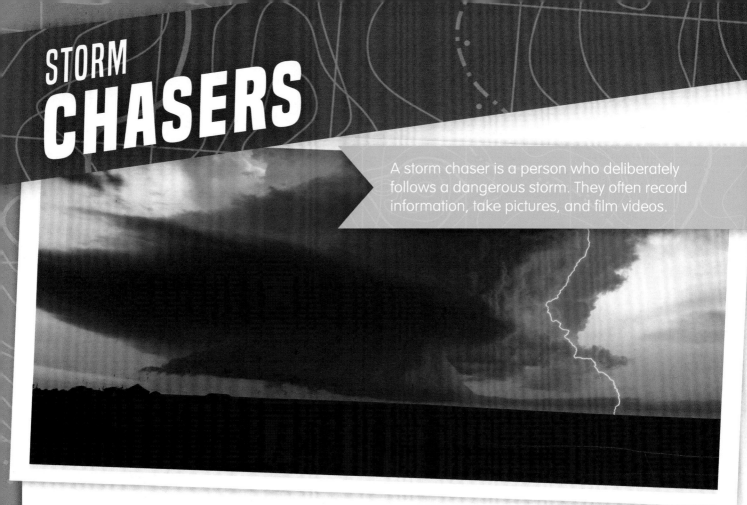

A storm chaser is a person who deliberately follows a dangerous storm. They often record information, take pictures, and film videos.

A Map for a Storm Chaser

Storm chasers use all sorts of maps to lead them to the storm. They might use forecasts from local weather stations to **pinpoint** a storm. One of the most important instruments for a storm chaser is radar. Radar creates a map of the surroundings and objects that are close by or far away. It does this by sending out radio waves, which bounce off objects and are reflected back. The radar can tell from the reflection of the waves what is out there. Storm chasers and weather stations use radar to pick up large clouds of rain and snow in the air. The Doppler on Wheels, or DOW, is a type of radar specially made for chasing storms. The DOW looks like a huge dish, and can be attached to the back of a truck.

A Doppler on Wheels Unit

CHASING STORM CHASERS

Online maps are made so they can change to display new information right away. The maps are usually **interactive**, so you can choose what sort of information you want to see. There are some maps on the Internet that track storms and storm chasers. A visitor to this kind of website can see a map with symbols moving around. Some of the symbols represent a storm chaser. If the visitor clicked on a storm chaser, they can see information about them, and maybe even a live video stream of what the storm chaser is filming.

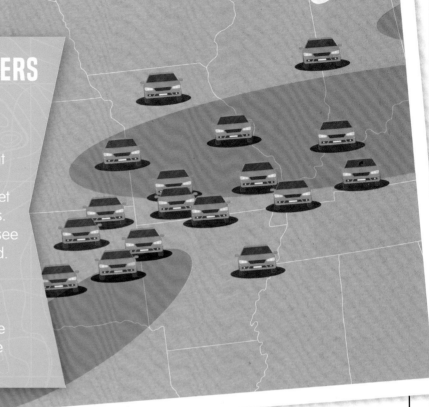

A Map of Storm Chasers

Storm chasing is extremely dangerous. Some storm chasers are scientists who are employed to record information, but some chasers are people who do it as a hobby. People who do this have an interest in extreme weather, but it's important to remember that chasing extreme weather is very dangerous. Although storm chasers mostly go after tropical cyclones or tornadoes, extreme weather also includes heavy blizzards, thunderstorms, and **dust devils**.

AVIATION WEATHER MAPS

Aircraft use a special sort of weather map called an aviation weather map. Vehicles that fly, like airplanes and helicopters, need lots of weather information, especially about the atmosphere high in the sky. If the movement of hot and cold air is creating dangerous weather, aircrafts may not be able to fly.

SEND IN THE CLOUDS

Aviation weather maps have a lot of symbols you would find on a normal weather map. There are warm fronts, cold fronts, isobars, wind speed and direction, and temperature. However there are also many other symbols. For example, areas of **turbulence** are shown with little peaks. Aviation weather maps also show areas with clouds. The height of the clouds from the surface of the Earth is called the cloud ceiling. An aviation weather map will show areas of different cloud ceilings.

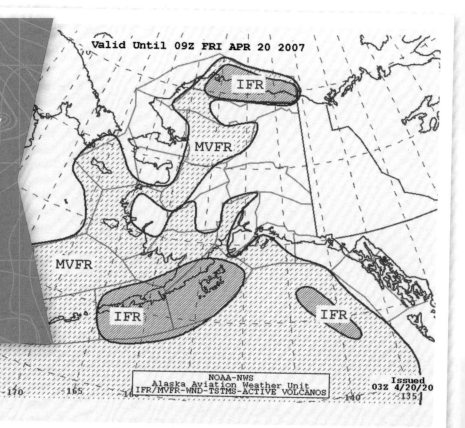

This is an aviation weather map. The red and blue areas show different types of low cloud ceilings.

Fly Another Day

Pilots must check aviation weather reports very carefully before they fly. Different aircraft are allowed to travel at different heights and in different weather. A pilot may be flying a small, one-person plane, which can't fly in areas of low cloud. The pilot must check to see if the weather conditions are too severe for the type of plane they are flying. Today, most aviation weather maps are found online, and might be posted every hour.

IN 2010, EYJAFJALLAJÖKULL CREATED A **PLUME** OF SMOKE THAT WAS 6.8 MILES (11 KM) HIGH.

FIRE AND ICELAND

Sometimes other things can affect an aviation weather report, such as natural disasters. For example, a volcanic eruption will shoot ash and smoke into the atmosphere. If it is a big volcano, there could be lots of material in the air, which makes it difficult to fly. On an aviation weather report, there will be a cloud-shaped symbol with "volcanic ash" written next to it. In 2010, a volcano in Iceland called Eyjafjallajökull (say: Ay-yah-fee-ad-layer-ker-tel) erupted. For several days a huge cloud of ash swept over Europe, and around 95,000 flights had to be canceled. Ash and smoke filled the air, as lava flowed out from **fissures** beneath the crater.

The ash from a volcanic eruption can drift a long way around the world. This map shows the ash cloud spreading from the 2010 eruption of Eyjafjallajökull.

THE SHIPPING FORECAST

STORMY SEAS

Aircraft are not the only vehicles that need to carefully listen to weather reports. Bad weather can make the sea very dangerous. To avoid danger, sailors regularly listen to the forecast to know which areas to stay away from. Some forecasts use a special, coded map to tell the sailors about the different parts of the sea.

THE SHIPPING FORECAST IS THE LONGEST RUNNING CONTINUOUS FORECAST IN THE WORLD, AND HAS BEEN GOING FOR OVER 150 YEARS.

A Radio Message

The Shipping Forecast is a radio program about the weather, and is broadcast from the **BBC** to boats in the waters around Britain and northwest and western Europe. The message goes out several times a day, with some of the messages being very late at night. The Shipping Forecast divides the waters around the United Kingdom into 31 areas. Each area has a special code name, such as Viking, Dogger, German Bight, and Humber. Each sailor knows which code name refers to which area of the map.

By mapping the areas in this way, the radio program can be very clear about exactly which parts of the sea have good or bad weather.

The Shipping Forecast follows the same strict order of areas each time, and is never more than 380 words long.

DOT MAPS

Some maps use dots to show where a type of thing is. Sometimes the dots show one place or building, and sometimes the dots show a group of things, like hundreds of people. Dot maps are a good way of seeing how things are spread out in an area.

Lake
Pond

Live Lightning

Dot maps can be useful when mapping some types of weather. Online lightning maps use dots to show lightning strikes around the world. These maps are live, which means they show the lightning strikes at the exact moment they are happening.

LINES, DOTS, ELECTRIC SHOCKS

The lightning maps are also interactive, which means the viewer is able to click on them and change settings or the information that is shown. The information is gathered from several weather stations, and settings can be changed to show night and day, or to only see lightning strikes from a certain time. The websites with lightning maps use Google maps and information from weather stations to create the interactive map you can see.

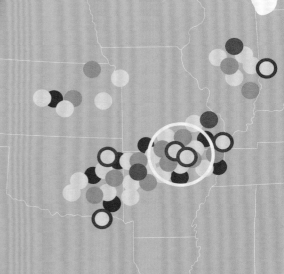

ANIMAL MIGRATION

What Is Migration?

Not all animals live in the same place all year round – many animals move from one location to another at different times of the year. This might be to breed or to find food. Lots of animals fly south during winter to **hibernate** or to find warmer weather. These movements are called migration.

WEATHER AND MIGRATION

Weather and climate are one of the main reasons that animals migrate. As our climate changes and the Earth's temperature slowly rises, it is likely that animal migration patterns will change in response to this. By looking at animal migrations, we can learn a lot about the world and the weather.

EVERY YEAR, AROUND 1.5 MILLION WILDEBEEST MIGRATE FROM TANZANIA TO KENYA (AND BACK AGAIN!) DUE TO SEASONAL RAINS AND IN SEARCH OF AREAS TO GRAZE.

These are some migration paths of the bar-tailed godwit bird. The bar-tailed godwit flies south from Alaska to New Zealand in autumn, and returns in spring.

BAR-TAILED GODWITS HAVE THE LONGEST NONSTOP MIGRATION OF ANY BIRD – 7,145 MILES (11,500 KM)!

TAGS AND TRACKING

Animals and insects travel very long distances during their migrations, so it is often very difficult to follow exactly where they are going. To help with this, scientists stick small tags or stickers onto the animals at the beginning of their migration route. These tags all have a unique code on them so the animal can easily be identified. If a person sees one of these animals with a tag on it, they can send the information to the scientists, who plot the animal's route onto a map.

Monarch butterflies are often tagged with small stickers so that their migration routes can be tracked.

Arctic Tern

The Arctic tern is a small bird that has the longest migration in the world. During the end of summer, Arctic terns fly from Greenland to Antarctica. When it is winter in the Northern Hemisphere, it is summer in the Southern Hemisphere. By flying south in September, the Arctic tern has a whole year of warm weather!

Northern Wheater
Arctic Tern
Amur Falcon
Ruff
Short-tailed Shearwater
Swainson's Hawk

This map shows the Arctic tern's migration compared to other birds' journeys.

SPACE WEATHER

A Forecast for Aliens

Earth isn't the only planet that has weather. There is a lot of strange weather throughout the solar system that would be impossible on Earth. Scientists map the weather on other planets by using robotic spacecraft, which travel the solar system and gather information. When a spacecraft nears a planet, it takes lots of different pictures. These pictures are sent back to Earth using radio waves, and are pieced together by computers and scientists. Eventually a full image is created of what the spacecraft saw.

WHAT KIND OF WEATHER DO OTHER PLANETS HAVE?

Spacecraft have taken pictures of Jupiter and found a giant storm raging on the planet's surface. The storm is two to three times the size of Earth, and has been going for over 400 years.

Spacecraft that have visited Neptune and Uranus have found that it probably rains diamonds. Scientists recreated the conditions of Neptune in a lab to show that this was true.

On Mars, there are dust storms that cover the whole planet, something that would never be seen on a planet like Earth.

SOLAR WIND

Aside from light, the sun also sends solar wind into space. Solar wind is made up of a flow of **charged particles**. The Earth is surrounded and protected from the solar wind by a magnetic field, which is also called a magnetosphere. Without the magnetosphere, Earth's atmosphere would be stripped away, and it would be impossible to survive.

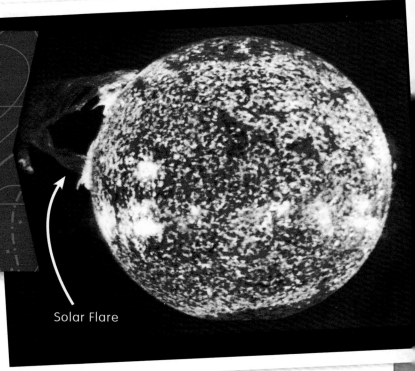

Solar Flare

Sometimes the sun sends out a burst of solar wind, which is called a solar flare. Solar flares are not usually dangerous, although satellites and spacecraft may be damaged.

The Auroras

In areas that are close to the poles, like the Arctic Circle or Antarctica, the solar wind interacts with the magnetosphere and bounces off the upper part of the atmosphere. Luminous, brightly colored lights are created. In the Northern Hemisphere, these lights are called the aurora borealis. In the Southern Hemisphere, the lights are called the aurora australis.

The Aurora Borealis

MAPPING THE AURORAS

People have created maps to make it easier to track and view the auroras. The maps show where the lights are likely to occur, and also have symbols for viewing sites and previous spots where the auroras were seen.

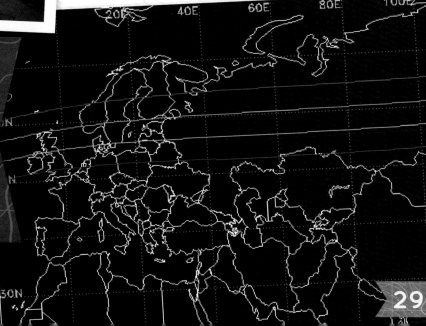

The aurora borealis can often be seen above the blue line.

RAINING ANIMALS

Bugs on the Screen

Over the years, weather stations have picked up some strange things while mapping the atmosphere with radar. Sometimes there seems to be no explanation for it. For example, in 2017, a Colorado weather station picked up a single, giant cloud of something on their radar. They did not know what this was.

After discussing the possibility it was birds, it eventually turned out it was probably a giant swarm of butterflies. Mapping the weather isn't always straightforward, even with all the technology we currently have.

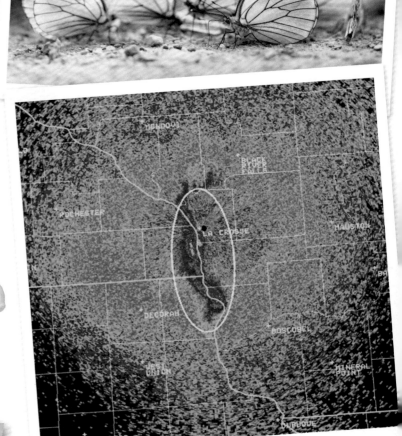

GET THE BIG UMBRELLA

There have been reports of raining animals throughout history. Although many of these cases might seem too strange to be true, reports are still made today. For example, in 2011, it apparently rained fish on a town in Australia called Lajamanu. Scientists still aren't sure what causes this, but they suspect it is some sort of violent storm that picks the animals up and carries them in the air to a faraway place. Nobody has made a map of this kind of weather...yet!

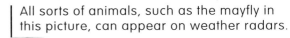

All sorts of animals, such as the mayfly in this picture, can appear on weather radars.

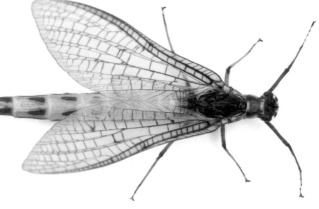

GLOSSARY

average	the most common or typical occurrence of something
BBC	British Broadcasting Company, an organization in the UK
Celsius	the metric measurement of temperature
charged particles	an atom or something smaller with an electric charge
charted	recorded on a map
currents	steady flows of water in one direction
dust devils	whirlwinds of dust
equator	the imaginary line around the Earth that is an equal distance from the North and South Poles
evaporates	turns from a liquid into a gas or vapor, usually through heat
evidence	facts and information that can prove if something is true or not
Fahrenheit	the imperial measurement of temperature
features	distinctive properties of the landscape
fissures	openings where something has split apart
hibernate	spend the winter sleeping or in a dormant state
interact	communicate and have an effect on each other
interactive	something that communicates and changes based on interaction
key	a part of a map that tells you what symbols or colors mean
landmarks	places or buildings that are famous or easily recognized
pinpoint	find or mark the exact location of something
plotted	drew a journey of something on a map
plume	long, tall cloud of smoke
radar	a piece of technology that senses the location of things using radio waves
radiometers	instruments that can detect radiation
satellites	machines in space that travel around planets, take photographs, and collect and transmit information
storms	violent or unstable parts of the atmosphere that cause bad or dangerous weather
temporary	only lasting for a short time
tilted	leaning to one side
tornado	a fast-moving, strong, and destructive wind that forms into a funnel shape
turbulence	shaky and unstable movement, usually of the air, which can affect airplanes

INDEX